VISIONS
OF
HAPPINESS

A poetic recollection of transformation
from pleasure and pain to purpose

Reshelle L. Matheny

Published by Warriors Talk, Inc.

ISBN: 978-0-578-71548-3

DISCLAIMER: This book contains adult content and language. It is not suitable for anyone under the age of 18 and may not be suitable for all adult readers. View at your own discretion. Language contained in this book may be offensive to some readers.

Printed in the United States of America

Edited by So It Is Written LLC

Cover design by Vixydesigns

First printing Edition 2019.

www.warriorstalk.org

Dedication

This book of poems **"Visions of Happiness"** is dedicated to anyone who has encountered pleasure and pain but has used it as fuel to walk in purpose.

TABLE OF CONTENTS

Acknowledgments

I would like to acknowledge my family, close friends and spiritual family for being encouraging and supportive through this journey called life.

To my inspirations, something good can come out of an unhappy situation.

To my Uncle EJ, Nancy (Lala) and David, you are deeply missed.

Thank you to SWJ and COJ for the inspired collaboration and poem contribution.

Thank you for witnessing my transformation as I transitioned from pleasure and pain to purpose.

Thanking God for allowing me to express and share my most inner thoughts.

Never allow anyone to erase your past, be it good or bad. The lessons we learn help shape our future.

Author's Notes

Being able to see myself *outside of myself* has allowed me to move forward in a way that pushes me to live on purpose with purpose.

I am not only a better person because of my storms and struggles; I am living in the moment and I am no longer haunted by my past hurts, disappointments and ill decision making. I encourage everyone reading this book of poems to find your own kind of happiness. Never let what's going on in other people's lives or around you to tap into your visions of happiness.

Introduction

Visions of Happiness is a book of
poems that takes you on life
transformations from pleasure and pain to
purpose. This journey has allowed me to
take on life's trials, tribulations and
celebrations, and transform them into
visions with purpose. As the reader, you
will be able to travel back in time and
venture off into this turbulent journey of
happiness.

The visions will connect you to your
own reality of highs, lows, love, faith and
disappointments — experiencing life-
altering events that keep you in a never-
ending loop and spiral you out into a world
of new beginnings.

~Chapter 1~
A Little Bitter, but Not Broken

A Little Bitter, but Not Broken

Years of bliss, and you said you see me in your future.
But at what capacity you don't know.
We shared everything—from a kiss, vacation and death
of loved ones, to the birth of a child.
A little bitter, but not broken.

After a night of passion, you kissed me goodbye as you
go off to work.
I skipped off to the bathroom, only to find a shrine filled
with lotion, potions, gels and crèmes—
all set up to make any woman scream.
But these weren't things I've ever seen.
A little bitter, but not broken.

A trip out of town for a job interview,
Only to get a call from your cell phone.
On the other end, a woman claiming she loves you.
I asked if you want this relationship open
so, you can have your heart's desires.
You replied, "No" and assured me I was your only one.
A little bitter, but not broken.

Wake up six months later

to a message on social media,

on how you were the love of her life.

But it wasn't your wife.

A little bitter, but not broken.

Wanting you to feel the pain the way I do,

I set off on my own love quest.

Only to bring forth a seed of love.

A seed that wasn't supposed to bloom, but it did.

Now you both know and hearts are broken.

A little bitter, but not broken.

I'm left with no one, but memories of what once was.

You can't stand to look at me.

Can't believe how fast things change.

There is a thin line between love and hate.

That line leads to your escape.

Together is not our destiny, nor fate.

Though it's all self-afflicted,

I'm still standing.

Thanking God for second chances.

A little bitter, but not broken.

All of Me

I gave all of me, mind, body and soul.
I allowed you to take control.
Control of my heart, hoping you wouldn't take it apart,
piece by piece, year after year.

My heart cannot take anymore.
Like a bomb, I'm ready to explode
into a million pieces; my heart, I can't control.

I gave you my all, in return for heartache and pain,
knowing that you would never change.
I gave you nights of passion,
hoping this would keep you wanting more.
In return, you left me bills,
bad credit and a pain in my heart that I can't restore.

I gave you my precious time,
knowing someday this would come to an end.
An end I didn't desire; but it came with the territory.
I gave you all of me, and the only thing
I'm left with is a story to tell —
wishing I could tell you to go straight to hell.

Today, I'm taking back all of me, along with the key to my heart. I'm putting it in storage for the next round. Only this time, I'm waiting patiently for the Father to do the choosing, knowing He will not send me someone Who will take …All of me.

Suddenly

Tender kisses in the night.
In your arms, I fit exactly right.
Whispering, "I love you" in my ear.
Yearning to taste your love and feel you near.

The phone rings and, suddenly, the mood erupts.
Suddenly, I feel cold and alone.
Your body is here with me, but I don't feel your touch.

Your mind has gone back in time
to that secret place you love so much.
Suddenly, your kisses do not feel so tender,
your arms so tight.
The words "I love you" have faded,
just as your presence in the night.

My heart hurts from your absence.
My body aches from the lack of your touch.
My mind wonders
why suddenly she matters so much.

No More

Dedicated to my big sister
Nancy "LaLa" Marshall:
I love you!

No more sunshine,
no more rain.
Praying and asking God to remove my pain.

No more neglect,
no more sorrow.
Wishing for a better tomorrow.

No more fears,
no more tears.
I've had my share down through the years.

No more looking back,
no more regrets.
I have a new home where I can finally relax.

Don't look at my past.
Look at me now,
for my soul is at peace.
I am with my Savior now.

Back in Time

Unhappy with life's choices.
Choices that bring me to a dark place —
A place I no longer recognize,
wishing I could go back in time.

All for self-gratification.
At the time, it seemed so satisfying.
Pleasing self was the only thing on my mind;
wishing I could go back in time.

Back in time to change my mind, my life, my destiny.
This is not what I dreamed life would be.
No fairytale ending for me.
All I have encountered is pure agony,
wishing I could go back in time.

Back in time, just to think things through.
For a small glimpse of "what if"
I had chosen to keep you.
Wishing I could go back in time.

~Chapter 2~
So High

So High

My eyes, my lips, my taste, my smell.

And boy, you know this body all so well.

Sitting here with my eyes closed, trying to replay the last

time we made love.

It's been too long since the last time we touched;

you know I just can't seem to get enough.

Enough of your tenderness; take me if you please.

I promise this time, I won't be a tease.

Wanting you every chance I get.

Not sure if this will be the last,

So, I got to get my fix.

Wanting every inch of you to be on every inch of me.

Boy, you know how to bring me to my knees.

Pleasing you is all I want to do.

This love is so strong, it leaves me paralyzed,

waiting for the next episode.

Waiting for time to pass while in recovery mode.

Wanting you more and more, overdosed, my body hits

the floor.

Taking a second to embrace my high while

shooting it up my veins,

this love is sure to drive me insane.

Satisfied is all I feel,

until my next fix.

This love is all surreal.

Holding On

Looking at you from a distance, hoping to catch your eye.
Praying no one notices just how much love we have inside.
Trying to justify why we are together when we know we should be apart.

Deep down, my heart knows that, someday, you will depart.
But I keep allowing you to enter,
preparing myself for what's to come —
in hopes of a little happiness and fun.

Waiting patiently on your call, hoping you have time for me.
Everyone else is allowed your attention, but me.

I just sit, waiting and watching, wanting to scream
"I love you!" into the crowd.
Fearing someone will hear me and question, I dare not.

Knowing we will get our time alone soon.
I just hold on until it's my turn to have you.

I enjoy every second we get, for I know our time is fading fast.

Only in my dreams will our love last.

Letting Go

Never thought this day would come.

The day when our hearts no longer beat as one.

There is no sunshine; only the rain is allowed here

because each drop hides my tears.

This was one of my biggest fears —

losing you.

Losing us.

Broken trust.

Letting go is my only option, and it's a must.

Knowing I'm partly to blame for my misery and pain.

Longing and wishing you would hold me again.

Who am I to pretend?

We both knew this love was destined to end.

I'm letting go; there's no need to hold on any longer.

My heart has turned to stone.

The love I once knew

 is so far gone.

Closure

It took a second to lose you,
and it will take a lifetime to get over you.

The pain is so hard to bear.
My heart, I wish I could spare.
Spare the pain of knowing we are through.

Reality has set in, and I no longer have you.
You have disappeared into the wind.
My heart trembles for fear of loneliness
and losing my best friend.

No longer able to get back a love that once was.
Twisted, shaken, brokenhearted and numb.

Longing to be in your presence, but afraid of the constant
rejection.

Alone at last, or at least moving on without me.
Together forever fading into eternity.
The curtain has closed, and the show is over.
Pride, envy and gluttony has set in.

Lust, anger, greed and sloth have become my best friends.

Still Standing

You leaving me was the best thing yet.
Tried so many times, but always walked away with
regret.

Not wanting to break our tie.
Fear of being without you,
I just hung on while I was dying inside.
So exhausted and love deprived.
Tired of trying with someone who never once allowed me
inside.
Inside your heart is where I longed to be.
Still standing!

Waiting on the day for you to open up your heart to me.
But that day never comes.
To you, this was a game.
We simply both had fun.
Still standing!

With my heart intact,
dreaming of this day,
wishing I could take it all back.
At a crossroads in my life,

not sure if I should go on
without you in my life.
Life will never be the same because losing you, I also
lose my friend.
Still standing!

Finding peace, knowing we will forever be connected
because of our seed.
The next time I fall in love, it will be reciprocated.
No longer wasting time on someone who isn't dedicated.
Dedicated to loving me with his mind, body and soul.

Lesson learned, and I'm moving on.
No more residue; my heart is on reserve.
Still standing!
Waiting on the love
I *deserve*!

~Chapter 3~
It's Not About Me

It's Not About Me

Today, I learn to appreciate what I have.
It's not about the money in my purse
or how fat my bank account is.
When it's all said and done,
it's my health that keeps me having fun.

It's not about the degrees on my wall.
One earthquake, and it's sure to fall.
It's not about the long locs
flowing from my beautiful head.
One bad perm, and it's sure to shed.

It's not about the sweet taste of my cookie,
the thickness of my thighs,
the roundness of my breast,
the juiciness of my lips
or the swing in my hips.
One night of deception without protection,
and you're sure to change your perception.

It's not about the label on my jeans.
It's not about my designer Choos.
It's not about the gas guzzlers sitting in my driveway.

It's not about the imported sofa in my living room.
It's not about the juicy steak and the Cristal on my table.

When it's all said and done,
it can be taken away within a blink of an eye, a strong
gust of wind, or one bad report from your physician.

This will have your heart wishing.
Wishing for another chance to make a difference when
your difference begins today.

It was never about me.
It is about the love in my heart.
The love I have for myself and my loved ones that
counts.
It's about appreciating life, the here and now.
Or what's it all about?

Never

Never say what a person won't do,
when they are in love with you.
Love makes you do some crazy things.

Some will lie, cheat, steal and even kill —
all in the name of love.
We are willing to risk our lives, our marriages, our bodies
— all for a piece of love.

Just to have a moment of happiness, we will sacrifice our
morals, Christianity
and sanity.

When the power of love takes over, no one can predict
our behavior.
Many of us are slaves to love and crave its flavor.

Love will make you think that you are not hurting
anyone.
That what you are doing is justified.
Love will make you an addict to stolen moments with
forbidden fruit.

We are willing to compromise our jobs, our finances and our peace of mind —
just because they said we were fine.
Not knowing we are headed for destruction in due time.
Never put anyone on a pedestal, but God.
He is the only perfect one.

Never say, "Never" when it comes to someone else's behavior.
When it's all said and done, we find ourselves doing the very thing we said we would *never do*.

Free

Set me free, so you can be as you want to be.

Don't lie to me and lead me on.

Don't take my heart on a joy ride.

I'm sick and tired of crying inside.

If you have a little love in your heart for me,

set me free, so you can be as you want to be.

Don't look into my eyes and tell me you love me.

Don't touch my soul, then turn around and leave a black hole.

I'm not as fragile as you think.

Set me free, so you can be as you want to be.

If you knew anything about me, you would know how strong I am.

Don't play with my love just to keep me as an option when all else fails.

I'm not the type to sit around every second, biting my nails and walking on eggshells.

Set me free, so you can be as you want to be.

Wondering when it's my turn to have you.

I'm sick and tired of playing the fool and being your
stepstool.
Set me free, so you can be as you want to be,
without me — *free*.

Shutting Down

If I can't depend on you,
then who?

If I call you, and you don't answer,
then what?

Seek and you shall find.
But, where are you?

Knock and the door shall open.
But you're not here.

There's a sick feeling in the air.
Do you even care?

The walls are caving in.
I can't find my friend.

I need a safe place to hide.
Trying to escape the fear,

Darkness hovers over.
There is a hollowness in the air.

The end is near,
and you're still nowhere near.

Counting on you was my only mistake.
Withdrawing my trust, Lord knows how much this heart
of mine can take.

Back to Reality

"I never felt this way before!"
At least that's what he told me.
Being in his arms is all so sweet.
I can't remember a time when I've been swept off my
feet.
Back to reality, this love is bittersweet.

Broken promises; I've heard it all before.
Just to get in my pants, you'll tell me more.
I thought you were different, even special.
But it was all part of your plan.
Back to reality, this love is like quicksand.

A plan to keep my head in the clouds, while you played
the role of your life.
You sure had me fooled into thinking I could someday be
your wife.
Boy, did I lose myself, but only for a little while.
Back to reality, this love is out of style.

You can't be satisfied with just one.
The favor is returned and, suddenly, this doesn't seem
fun.

Now, you're the one left brokenhearted.

Wonder if any of this was true.

Back to reality, this equation no longer includes you.

Can't bear the thought of moving on without you.

The pain is unbearable.

Can't seem to catch my breath.

Watching you with her is for sure a slow death.

But I've got to find a reason.

Back to reality, this love is out of season.

~Chapter 4~
Sunshine

Sunshine

Sunshine, rain or snow,

he loves me.

This I know.

Trials and tribulations,

outraged at the lack of participation.

Bill collectors, lack of funds;

this love isn't for everyone.

Sunshine, rain or snow,

he loves me.

This I know.

Years passing, aged skin …

Where in the hell does love fit in?

Jealousy, insecurities and pride …

What the hell is on his mind?

Sunshine, rain or snow,

he loves me.

This I know.

Baby after baby, you think I would have learned with the

first one.

Blessings come in all shapes and sizes.

I am grateful to have some.

Sunshine, rain or snow,

he loves me.

This I know.

A house, car and vacation are all in the plans.

When I ask, just hold on, until you find yourself fading

fast.

Sunshine, rain or snow,

he loves me.

This I know.

Time has run out; no seconds left on the clock.

He is still making promises just to keep me on lock.

Sunshine, rain or snow,

he loves me.

This I know.

How did you do it?

You taught me a true lesson.

Intoxicated by your essence,

dumb, silly, crazy in love.

Your smile shines brightly, like the sun above.

You walk into a room and steal the show.

I melt like butter in your hand, nice and slow.

To watch you undress is like watching a movie

with anticipation wanting you to do me.

I take you in my pudding and mix it well.

I like the way you stir with your spoon; you can tell.

Your moans, shakes, the way you smell,

the way you taste with all of it combined.

It's too much for me to handle and it blows my mind.

What did you drug me with?

For it is, you I adore.

This love feels good,

so, give me more.

You got me sprung out!

How did you do it?

So Good

Our eyes connected, and nothing else needs to be said.
Seconds later, we are caressing each other intensely on
the bed.

As we come up for air, you gently stroke my hair.
Quickly sink your teeth into my soft brown skin.
Never knew pain could feel so good.

Almost like a sin,
you keep reeling me in.
As my eyes rolled back into my head,
my lips shiver and I slowly whisper,
over and over again,
"This right here is so good."

My body tingles with every touch, every kiss, with every
breath, wishing this would last forever.
As you continuously glide inside while gripping my
thighs, juices flow slowly, but surely.
Eyes rolled back into my head,
my lips shiver and I slowly whisper,
over and over again,
"This right here is so good."

Just as I open my eyes, you disappear
and I am left with the smell of you, lingering in the air.
My body waits patiently on your return,
anticipating our bodies reuniting
as one.

Eyes rolled back into my head,
my lips shiver and I slowly whisper,
over and over again,
"This right here was so good."

Until Then

Knowing you love me is enough to carry me to our next encounter.

I long to see your face, hear your voice and taste your lips.

I can't get enough of you, wishing I had you at my fingertips.

Wanting more of you every day, so you can feel the rhythm in my hips.

Knowing our time together is restricted.

Till we meet again, remember the softness, but juiciness of my lips.

The gyration of my hips and the sweet taste of my grips.

Our Time

Midnight finally arrives.
It's our time again; the time when our souls become one.
I'm waiting patiently just to see you.
In my arms is where you will lay,
me kissing every inch of your face.

Caressing you from head to toe,
trying not to let my love explode.
You tell me you love me and miss me so.
I hang on to every word, wanting more.
More of you, till my body is in overdose.
You are the one who's in control,
so, guide me to our next episode.

Just then, the doorbell rings
Breathless, heart palpitating and weak at the knees,
trying to hold back my excitement.
As I reminisce on the many ways you aim to please,
anxiously, I open the door —
only to hear you say,
"Baby, your feet must be tired
because you've been running through my mind all day."

Black see-through cami, thongs and 5-inch stilettos.

He immediately starts kissing, licking and caressing

in places I didn't know existed.

Just then, his head disappeared into my pool of love.

I started to shake as he pulled me in closer.

Our bodies fit like a hand in glove.

Just as I pulled out protection,

he lost his erection.

Said he couldn't get no satisfaction

with his love all wrapped up.

It's a distraction.

A text message came through,

he quickly hopped into the shower.

I tried not to notice the song:

There Goes My Baby by Usher.

It's not ours.

Trying to be a good woman and not snoop,

but my woman's intuition tells me to read it

so, I can get the scoop.

"I enjoyed our night of love.

Your hands are tantalizing.

Your tongue is mesmerizing."

Just then, he appeared, body dripping wet.

I pressed send

just as he leaned in to kiss my lips.

I asked, "Baby, do you love me?"

He replied, "Yes!"

"Baby, am I your only one?"

He replied, "Yes!"

I picked up his phone and said, "Hello Wifey, did you get all that?"

I Will

As long as you're being led by God,
I will follow you.

As long as you're consistently seeking God,
I will follow you.

As long as you're attempting to get it right on a daily
basis,
I will follow you.

Even in those times when you fall short,
I will follow you.

When your strength is depleted from carrying the weight
of the world on your shoulders,
I will cover you.

When the world beats you down with their words and
negativity,
I will cover you.
When opportunity lacks and passes you by,
I will cover you.

When you have given your best, and it just ain't good enough,
I will cover you.

When you're tired, weak and weary, and all hope seems lost,
I will be your strength.

When darkness is before you and you can't see the light of day,
I will trust you.

When the curtain has closed, the cheering is no more and the crowd has faded,
I will follow you.
I will cover you.
I will submit to you.
I will trust you.
I will be your muse.
I will love you.
I will pray for you …
And God will see you through.

My King

He walked into my life like a thief in the night and stole
my heart away.
We talk, we laugh, we kiss and make love till the break of
day.

Just as I was feeling like I was slipping away,
 he came and opened my heart, my mind,
my soul and made me feel whole.
Who is this man who I adore?

The man who treats me like a queen.
 In his thighs, I lay between,
caressing every inch of his manhood.
With my lips and fingertips anticipating an eruption.

 My mouth waters with just the thought of him touching
me in places I didn't know existed.
His lips discovered my treasure,
And, boy, can this man bring me pleasure.

 Who is this man I crave?
He is an awesome father, lover and friend.
To him, I will always give in.

Into his web of lustful sins, as he slips in.

Into my basket of tasteful fruit, this man is in heaven with every bite.

Just being in his company is a delight.

Whenever we are apart, it's his absence that gets me in a fright.

He is the one I'm longing to hold tight.

So tight that I don't dare to let go,

for this man is my King.

~Chapter 5~
Love Is

Love Is

Love is …
Being in sync with your feelings and never having to ask.

Love is …
No matter what other people are in the room, you are the center of attention.

Love is …
Holding me in your arms and listening to the beat of our hearts drum as one.

Love is …
Being two worlds apart and never having to doubt our love.

Love is …
Being able to forgive the one you love, even through the pain.

Love is …
Looking past the cause and working through the effects.

Love is …

No matter how long it's been since the last time we touched, reuniting feels surreal.

When a Man Loves a Woman

When a man loves a woman, there is nothing that he
wouldn't do.
He will cross a river just to get to you.
He will never think twice about putting you first
because he knows the love that he receives in return will
always quench his thirst.

When a man loves a woman, he will work, day and night,
just to keep food on the table, a roof over her head and a
silent night.
He will never kiss and tell,
for he knows how to keep a secret well.
Longing to hold her in his arms in hopes of eternity. He
gives her his heart in return for her intimacy.

When a man loves a woman, you see,
 he will go to the end of the earth and back
just to get a glimpse of her beauty.
 For he knows if trouble arises, she is the one who got his
back.
He's the only one that knows just how to bring her sexy
back.

Never lifting a finger to harm her or a voice to intimidate her.

He talks to her with passion and handles her with gentleness.

When a man loves a woman, he knows the recipe to love.
There is no other explanation
this man must be sent from heaven above.

What is Love

Love doesn't bring on a struggle.

Love doesn't hurt you.

Love wants the best for you.

Love wants to give you the best.

What is love?

Love feels your pain and comforts you.

Love makes you a priority.

Love allows you to express your feelings.

Love doesn't want you to suffer.

What is love?

Love is like the mist in the air after rain on a hot summer's night.

Love is acknowledging the other person's feelings and not shutting them out.

Love is compromise, without regret.

Love is giving up a little to gain a lot.

What is love?

Love is being honest with yourself, as well as others.

Love is the person you see in the mirror every day.

Love yourself before you can share that love with someone else.

You Are

Did you ever know that you are patient, honest and thoughtful?

Did you ever know that you are hard-working, caring and playful?

Did you ever know that you are a good lover and my friend?

You are always there for me.
From the moment we met, your love has kept me afloat.
You are the one who comforts my heart and keeps it at ease.
You are the only one I aim to please.

Everyone needs someone to listen to.
Everyone needs someone to lean on.
Everyone needs someone's shoulder to cry on.
Everyone needs someone to make them a priority.
Everyone needs someone to make them see that
tomorrow is a better day.
Everyone needs someone to make them feel sexy.
Everyone wants to feel adored.

Everyone wants to feel loved.

I feel as though the world will stop spinning if you stop loving me.

Did you know that you were this to me?

Did you ever know that you mean everything to me?

But this is not where you want to be.

I Love You Beyond

I love you beyond your hurt, insecurities and flaws.
I love you beyond your distrust, uncertainties and those
times you fall.

I love you beyond your heaviness, actions and your call.
I love you beyond your hugs, kisses and passion,
which has the potential to heal us all.

I love you beyond your actions, intellect and emotional
walls.
I love you beyond your purpose, dreams and goals.

Looking for love in all the wrong places,
adapting to the hearts of every encounter.

A chameleon at its best, trying to mask the hurt.
If you're looking for unconditional love, look to the
Father.

As much as the human heart can bear, without exploding,
my love for you is continuously unfolding.

The One Who Has My Heart

The one who has my heart
knows how to make the rain stop
and bring out my sunshine.

The one who has my heart
shields me from danger
and knows how to control
his anger.

The one who has my heart
knows how to fight temptation
when we're apart.

The one who has my heart
knows no other can replace
me in the dark.

The one who has my heart
knows I would never betray his love,
but do everything to preserve it.
The one who has my heart
knows that I would do anything,
including taking his last name

and wearing his ring.

The one who has my heart
shares our seed planted by our love.
The one who has my heart was sent from above.

Someone to Love Me

I want someone to love me for me.
Someone who only wants to be with just one.
Someone to walk with in the rain and help ease my pain.
Someone who treasures our time,
while enjoying the sunshine.

Someone to kiss me in a crowd and say, "I love you!" out
loud and not care who is looking or listening.

I want someone to love me for me.
Someone to take their time and make sweet, gentle love
to me and not be afraid of our intimacy.
Someone who is willing to explore the many ways to my
treasures
and keep me wanting more of his pleasures.

I want someone to love me for me.
Someone to hold me in their strong, but tender arms so
close that we can hear our hearts beating as one.
Someone to dance with me after the music is done.
Someone who will not play with my heart,
one who is trustworthy from the start.

I want someone to love me for me so that we can feel
free, from now until eternity.

I want someone to love me for me.
Someone to change my last name, turn in his player's
card while protecting my heart.
Someone who embraces my seeds as their own.

I want someone who appreciates the options,
but stays true to his queen.
Someone who's worthy of my loyalty and
submissiveness.
Never abusing it or taking it for granted, but leading me
to the Creator.

I want someone to love me for me,
in all my authenticity.
I want someone to love me for me so that we can feel
free, from now until eternity.

~Chapter 6~
Together We Can

Together We Can

I can't keep calm!
I love my black men.
Inside and out,
you are more than a shell with skin.

Together, we create life.
Together, we will preserve it.

United as one,
please put down the guns.

It will take more than a bullet to wipe out God's plan.

Know this to be true:
I love *you*, black man.
You will not be extinct.
Keep pushing forward
with your master plan.

While your future resides safely in God's hands.
I love you, black man.
Together, we can conquer the land.

Blaque Woman, I am NOT for sale

My tight, black curly hair and my broad nose.
My full lips and my wide hips.
Making babies, but never losing my grip.
Blaque woman, I am *not* for sale.

Ignore me when others are around.
Degrade my existence,
try to erase my history.
Exposing everything,
leaving nothing as a mystery.
Blaque woman, I am *not* for sale.

Leaving me feeling unlovable,
no longer a desire to be around.
My independence intimidated you.
I'm no threat, yet I'll always have your back.
I hold you down when no one else is around.
Blaque woman, I am *not* for sale.

Treating me like I'm from the clearance rack,
I'm not discounting my worth.
My dignity is not for sale.
I come with a high price,

far more than any gem or precious stone.

Blaque woman, I am *not* for sale.

I am a mother, sister, daughter and your backbone.

When you look in the mirror, you see me.

I birth you.

You are me.

My black is beautiful for all see.

A size 2, 4, 6, 10 or 12.

Light, dark, caramel or pale-skinned.

 We are all made in His image

and He paid the price.

Laying down his life,

an ultimate sacrifice.

Blaque woman, I am *not* for sale.

Black Man, I See You

I've seen your tears, pain and frustration down through
the years.
Climbing to the top, only to get knocked back down.
Treated like a clown,
always looking for ways to tear you down. Feeling alone,
like no one has your back.
Constantly being disrespected and distracted, all to get
you off track.
Black man, I see you.

Backed into a corner while trying to survive.
Shot down in the street like a dog by one of your own.
Constantly being told you are worthless.
Scrambling to stay on your feet,
not realizing you were born packing heat.
Black man, I see you.

You were given all the tools to succeed,
but your environment keeps you in a strain.
Long life seems hard to obtain.
They won't let you breathe,
shackles constantly on your feet.
Black man, I see you.

Pushed to the limits,

dropping like flies in these streets.

Keep fighting and pushing.

Never let them see you sweat.

Never let them see you quit,

you were created for this.

Black man, I see you.

Warrior, king and Supreme Being.

Make a stand.

Take a stand,

 and stand for something.

 Stand for freedom,

 to be all God created you to be

with the world at your feet.

Black man, I see you.

Dear Black Men, You Are

Impregnable

Undefeated

Unassailable

Unconquerable

Inviolable

Unshakable

Invincible

Indestructible

Intoxicating

Impenetrable

Exhilarating

Extraordinary

Invigorating

Influential

Incomparable

Dominant

Necessary

Loving

Supreme

King

Black men, you are all those things.

Black men, you hold the key to unlock the door.

The door to obtain the impossible

with God as your guide.

You can walk, head held high, with a strut in your stride.

Erasing all labels, knowing exactly what you bring to the table.

Never folding, but always in control of your destiny.

Black men, you were created to reign supreme,

to rise above all that they called you to be.

Black men, you are powerful.

When you know the power you possess,

you are unstoppable.

Then, and only then, will you rise above the negativity.

Be what God created you to be.

Be who God created you to be.

Black men, you are *not forgotten*!

Good Black Man

A good black man is one who loves God and has a
connection with God.
One who is able to pray for me and with me!
Who can cover me when I am not able to do it myself!

A good black man is one who is up for the challenge of
trying, every single day, to achieve his goals and dreams.
One who shares them with me and allows me to buy into
his vision to help make it a reality.

A good black man recognizes his flaws,
but embraces them to strengthen him moving forward.
He is selective in the company he keeps.
He never allows drama or past hurts to keep him from
loving the one that's before him.

 He is an awesome provider and protector.
He is consistently making provisions for the one he loves.
He is confident in his manhood and his existence here on
earth.
 He is a lover of his community and strives to invoke
wisdom, knowledge and God's Word to those who appear
to be lost.

He is loving and gentle, yet firm with his interactions
with me.
He includes me in the details of his life.
I am a priority, not an option.
He is intentional about his love for me.
He reminds me constantly through his actions and words
that he appreciates me.

A good black man has a relationship with his children
and family, and he accepts my children as his own.

He is drawn to success and continues to get back up when
his falls.
He knows he has a good black woman to fill in the gaps
when he calls.

He is very transparent with me and honest about his
intentions with me.
He doesn't have time for games because he's too busy
loving me, creating a dynasty and legacy for his kids.

He's not afraid to allow his helpmeet to pursue her
dreams, and he does everything to support me.
He is my #1 fan and I am his.

Together, we create an unbreakable bond that is God-centered and love-filled.

This good black man is filled with integrity, compassion and humility. He is not afraid to admit when he is wrong.

I am capable of ushering him into his God- ordained ministry with my patience, love, support and forgiveness when needed.

I create a stress-free environment for him to be creative and perform at the top of his game.
Where he lacks, I definitely fill in.
When he is tired and weak, I rejuvenate him so that he can reign supreme.
This strong, sexy, intelligent black man is my *king*.

A Prayer for Our Black Men

Father God,

I ask that you send a covering over our black men.
Allow justice to be served for all those responsible for
taking innocent lives.

 I pray that you raise the standard in our black men,
so that the rest of the world will see their worth.

I pray that you open their eyes and show them how
important it is to be in their children's lives.

I pray that black men will rise up and be a shield of
protection for their seeds mentally and physically.

I pray black men have a spiritual awakening, go into
warfare and take back our communities.

I pray black men come to see how vital it is to start their
own businesses and create generational wealth.

I pray black men abandon the practices of investing in material items that put money in the pockets of those who do not invest in their future and could care less if they have one.

I pray, Lord, that you allow black men to band together in unity to protect, educate and empower each other.
To value not only their lives, but the lives of others.

I pray that black men see value in their presence in the lives of their women and children.

I pray that black men come to realize that, in their absence, the black family is not complete.

I pray that our black men look at the long-term consequences of their actions and how it all plays a part in how others see you and treat you.

 Finally, my prayer is for black men to totally surrender to you, Lord, and allow you to direct their path.

In Jesus' name,

Amen!

Make America Great Again

Apologize for the delay.
Had to get my little ones squared away.
Let's get to the task at hand —
make America great again.

Never has,
never will,
trying to operate in God's Will.
Trust issues with the prophet;
now we're dead out of options.

Democratic or Republican,
can we get along with our fellow man?

Election rigged!
Threaten to deport the Mexicans!
Building a wall, while watching America fall.
Wasting time on empty challenges,
seeing who can do the best running man or mannequin.
Channel that energy toward eradicating systems used to
oppress the man.

Heartless, cruel, with a fat bank account.
Won't get you into heaven.
No need to shout,
stumbling through life, wondering if it's all real.

Try burying a child before his 18th birthday,
while watching the blues get away.
Running around town, dodging clowns.

If voters knew the truth before going to the booth,
all would become familiar with the process,
only to be told some nonsense.
Expecting us to forget our daunting past is a hard pill to
swallow.

It made us who we are today — resilient, humble,
optimistic and some, hollow.
Moving forward with the grace of God,
if we try to accept and go a little more in-depth,
maybe then we can find that heavenly state of mind.

From, "Yes, We Can!" to making America "great again,"
it's true that we are stronger together,
but only God can get us there.

A piece of divine can be hard to find when you don't keep that peace inside.

Closing my eyes, wishing it was just a dream.

Now I lay me down to sleep,

Obama's out and Hillary has met defeat.

Trumps wins.

Could this be the end?

Stay tuned as he makes America "great again."

~Chapter 7~
Wounded Warrior

Wounded Warrior

As I lie in my bed, knowing that I could've been dead,
tears shed.
Shedding weight, wondering if it's here again,
trying to bring me to an end.
Living my life free from fear;
trying so hard to get this devil out my ear.

Thinking positive, that's what they say.
But how when he's riding my back day by day?
Not wanting to feel paranoid, insane or ashamed.
So, I hide within me and take the blame.

How could I be so reckless and not catch this?
Wondering daily, what did I do to deserve this?
Was it my lack of faith or trust in Him?
Was it my unfaithfulness and not living totally for Him?
Is He trying to get my attention to bring me closer to
Him?

To depend totally on Him, not man?
Is this His will, that I suffer and be ill?
Or is He just trying to get me to be still?

Still enough to hear His voice and follow His directions.

Still the unknown haunts me day after day.

Sitting, waiting and praying, it doesn't take me away.

Watching tears flow down my face,

can't help but wonder if today is the day.

Keymo Dayzze

Aching bones, loose teeth, chocolate skin.
What the hell is happening?
Black fingernails smelling of crusty sores,
Wondering, how much more?

Toxic dripping into my veins, hour after hour,
waiting to kill cells is enough to drive anyone insane.
The pain of sores in my mouth has caused me to lose
weight and look paper thin.

No appetite.
No relief in sight.
I can't fathom why this journey began.
Trying to hold on when I have every reason to let go.
Seeing those little eyes looking up at me,
brings me to my knees.
Praying and asking my heavenly Father to preserve me.

Growing old, wanting to see my seeds in bloom.
Popping pills, hoping to eliminate the residue.
Finding strength I never knew.
Life goes on, until the good Lord sees fit.
Celebrating life day by day as my beauty fades away.

Hair shedding, like rain falling immensely from the sky.

The rain hides my tears as they disappear into thin air.

Paralyzed by the collateral damage.

Searching for a better tomorrow.

Blood running thin, so doc had to pump some in.

Life has a way of humbling you to bring you to praise.

Praise for the things past, present and future.

Knowing what's to come is better than what's been.

So, I hold on with all my might,

Keeping hope on these sleepless nights.

Praying to my heavenly father to erase the stains of these chemo days.

Sweet Victory

Breast cancer has impacted my life,
forcing me to live every day on purpose, with purpose.
No longer sitting on the sidelines, watching everyone else
live out their dreams.

It's paralyzed me temporarily and erased my outer
beauty,
only to replace it with a canvas,
waiting for the artist to create a better version of me.
All while embracing sweet victory.

Breast cancer took me out of my comfort zone
and put me in a zone
where I was forced to create my own
reality of sexy, normal and happy.

It made my family rally around me as they showered me
with support.
Cheering me on every step of the way.
The impact was devastating, but I was able to bounce
back with every ounce of fight in me.
All while embracing sweet victory.

Continuously rising above life's trials and tribulations thrown at me.
Being able to stand and straighten my crown that my King has presented to me.
Never giving up or giving in.
Keeping a tight grip and pushing toward the win.
All while embracing sweet victory.

A thriver that holds on and never folds.
A survivor of storms attempted to erase me.
A warrior by trade is what they call me.
A conqueror by birth is what was granted to me.
All while embracing sweet victory.

Total Healing

Leaving me empty, dazed and confused,
this storm fueled the warrior within.
No longer a bystander; instead,
I'm soaring with the wings of a conqueror.

Trusting, depending and believing
 in my Creator to pull me through.

Counting on the rainbow
 after the storm that illuminates the
spirit within me.

Total healing, I pray for
physically, mentally and spiritually.

Leaving me free and empty,
for my Creator to use me as He pleases.

Previvor, co-survivor, survivor or thriver,
we're all equal in God's eyes.
Walking in favor, saved by grace.
Praying while slaying giants,
landing them on their face.

And, in the midst of my prayers,

total healing is what was granted to thee.

Unstoppable

What makes you unstoppable?
Wait and see how you feel when I'm finished with you.
You're no better than Job.
He lost everything.
I don't have to remind you about Eve,
who was easily deceived.
You're no different.
What makes you untouchable?

I'll have you locked up in the prison of your mind,
worrying and contemplating death.
Unable to eat or think, on top of that.
You'll never get a good night's sleep.

Inflict you with disease, where the pain is unbearable.
Dying inside physically, paralyzed mentally,
and starve you spiritually.
You will be afraid to look at your own shadow.
Head hung so low that you will become unrecognizable.

The voices in your head,
attempting to tear you to shreds,
poisoning your mind with self-doubt.

Robbed your loved one
and pushed them to an early grave.
Have you grieving so hard that you will forget your
name.

I'll steal your innocence,
and leave you dazed and confused.
Have you lost for years,
trying to erase the residue.
Afraid to look in the mirror,
not liking what you see.

So, you still think you're unstoppable?

Well, wait and see!
I won't give up. I won't give in.
I was born in turbulence,
odds stacked against me.
They were expecting me to lose.
Homeless to CEO, I'm uncontrollable.

Standing in a field of uncertainty,
 God stepped in and rescued me from the hands of the
adversary,
only to be saved by the one who erased all my pain.

Self-love don't come easy.

Trying to fit in while dealing with rejection.

Questioning the skin I'm in,

Never giving in.

Instead, you take the win.

Reminded myself that I'm a child of the King.

Winning is in my DNA.

I'm an undisputed queen.

When you finished talking,

everything you mentioned was a thing of the past.

Moving on with purpose, knowing trouble don't last.

Leaving fear behind me as I blaze the trail.

Now what's the question you asked me?

Oh, yeah! What makes me unstoppable?

Well, you see, I'm remarkable.

I serve a God who's *unstoppable*.

Say It Ain't So

Say it ain't so!
This monster has knocked at my door.
There is no room for you to live here.
But he has already multiplied and divided.
He's already laid his roots,
Hoping none would be the wiser.

Found it in Vegas while in the shower.
Quickly turned my life sour,
upside down and into a whirlwind.
To my knee I go, asking for deliverance from sin.
Forgive me, save me, cleanse me,
preserve me, heal me and make me whole.

Give me a second chance
to see my seeds bloom.
Embrace my wrinkles and gray hairs.
Life just doesn't seem fair.
Where is my fairytale ending?

Instead, I'm having poison implanted into me.
Killing off cells,
Feeling like I'm in hell.

Life goes on with or without me.
Bracing myself for what's to come.

Preparing for war,
this is one battle I can't win alone.

So, I keep hoping, praying and pushing
until the victory is mine.
With my Creator by my side and faith in His plan,
this is one test I won't fail.
This monster doesn't stand a chance in hell.

~Chapter 8~
My End to New Beginnings

My End to My Beginnings

We've known from the beginning
that this day would come.
Was good while it lasted;
I sure had fun.
Trying to hold back my tears
as I unleash my fears.
Distorted by all the wasted years,
while you planned your exit.

One last look into your deep brown eyes.
One last touch of your soft, sexy brown skin.
One last juicy kiss from your full, but firm lips.
I just can't seem to get enough.
Never dreamed of us parting this way.
The pain is too tough.

All the things we took for granted, I will soon miss
This is the happiest I've been in a long time.
Then, reality sinks in and you're no longer mine.
I keep telling myself it's not over.
Watching you walk out the door for the last time
is for sure closure.

New Beginning

I love his confidence.
I love the way he has embraced himself.
I love his intelligence
and his thirst for knowledge.

I love the way he handles me — firm, but gentle.
I love the compassion he has in his heart.

I love the beautiful music he makes.
My heart trembles with each beat,
knowing that our next encounter will be ever so sweet.

I'm in love with his brain.
Can't wait to hear him speak.
Watching the words flow from his lips
sends my mind off into the deep,
deep end of the world,
Wondering if, *"One day, I'm gonna be his girl!"*

If only for a moment to be in his arms.
Making our own sweet music.
Never touching until our souls united as one.
Dancing to the music, this love has just begun.

My Soul Mate

Tall, dark and handsome.
Skin so smooth that it feels like butter.
Lips so full and soft, but firm,
when pressed against mine.

His head shines so brightly in the night light.
Arms open wide, waiting to hold me tight.
So tight that I sink in, into his deep brown eyes.

His smell is dreamy and drives me wild.
All the while, whispering the sounds of passion in my
ear.
All the things I love to hear.

His voice is like a trumpet,
ringing so loud.
It's no wonder my head is in the clouds.
This time, I choose not to come down.

High is where I want to be.
Only he can bring me to my knees,
and he's the only man I aim to please.

Skin glistening with every touch,
it's no wonder why I love this man so much.

When I'm not in his presence, my soul aches,
longing to feel the warmth of his embrace.
Sagacity tells me he's the one.
Curtain closed; my search is complete.
At last, my soul mate and I are one.

King

My king, his queen.

My covering, his helpmeet.

My Lord, His servant.

My protector, his peace.

My provider, his ego.

My teacher, his student.

My lover, his fulfillment.

My quarterback, his cheerleader.

My front, his backbone.

My eagle, his prey.

My main course, his dessert.

My friend, his confidant.

My Zeus, his muse.

My lover, his wife.

My husband, my king.

I Deserve

I deserve a love that is true.
I deserve to have my cake and eat it, too.
Feeling down and blue is not living.
Someone always taking, never giving.

I put my heart on the line one too many times,
only to have it snatched out and brewed like coffee
grinds.

Some say love is blind.
Truth is, love plays tricks on the mind,
always leaving me behind.
Behind the walls of shame,
determined to drive me insane,
like hair dye leaving stains.
I deserve a love that is true.
I deserve to have my cake and eat it, too.

This love war is no joke.
Doctor said I'm borderline for a stroke.
Stroking me is all he wants to do,
leaving traces of him in my love pool.
Treating me more and more like a fool,

with every deposit, I'm left confused.

While he's attempting to erase my muse
with mental and verbal abuse,
I'm trying effortlessly to break this soul tie
with thoughts of suicide.
Trying to ease my mind, this isn't love.
It's worse than genocide.

He's trying to keep my love confined.
My love is like an eagle, destined to soar.
He's realizing he no longer holds the key
to keep me from wanting more.
Broke loose from his mental chains,
I'm free to love again.

I deserve a love that's true.
I deserve to have my cake and eat it, too.

Residue!

I was smitten day one but kept it movin'.
Played that organ; kept it grooving.

Days and the weeks just snuck on by,
Till I finally had the nerve to give her a try.

Chocolate never looked so good.
Naw, I never thought it would.
It's so true: the darker the berry, the sweeter the "juice."
I wanted her badly.
I wanted her "loosed."

My joy was to give her my mind, body and soul.
I want her to have no remorse, but to take control.

But there he was, doing Da Dew.
Walking in and out, leaving residue.
Yet, I'm left home alone, asking, "Why?"
I went to first base, then second came.
Bout to hit a home run but missed my aim.
Telling her, "It's okay," but knowing it's a lie.

Pushed away again, keeping me at bay.

Again, back in jail; can't come out to play.

Nice guys *do* finish last. But geesh! Why me?

I mean, I been so patient,

and we feel so free.

She's afraid I'll walk away, like other men do.

But if I just had *all* of her, like she got me, too.

That next level is the place I wanna be.

This level is nice, but I'm getting old, ya see.

Why can't she see what I see? I need my boo!

On 1-10-15, she was free. No more residue.

I need to hear that song, soon, irresistible.

Wait! What is it again? Is it unthinkable?

My Soul Mate II

Back into my life.
Only this time, it's different.
My soul mate, the one my soul aches for.

We met at our usual place,
anticipating your warm embrace.
My soul mate, the one I prayed for.

Our walks seem endless.
Our talks know no limits.
My soul mate, the one I longed for.

The sound of your voice is sweet music to my ears,
Melting all my deepest fears.
My soul mate, the one I hold dear.

We became one at a tender age.
Just like Burger King, you had it your way.
My soul mate, the one I adore.

I need you in my life.
Wrapped in your arms in hopes of making it seem real.
My soul mate, the man of my dreams.

Wondering if any of this was real.

Not having you in my life is definitely surreal.

I Deserve Part II

I deserve a love that's true.
I deserve my cake and to eat it, too.
Second chance, in hopes all would be better.
He made promises to make it last forever.
Sick and tired of being sick tired,
my heart strings have been played like a puppet.

I deserve a love that's true.
I deserve my cake and to eat it, too.
Giving you the best I've got,
 only to come up empty every time.
Wine and dine faded in the night.
Quality time became a thing of the past.
Trying to fit me now sure didn't last.

I deserve a love that's true.
I deserve my cake and to eat it, too.
A priority, I am not.
He barely makes time or pencils me in.
Action speaks louder than words.
Staying in this relationship is absurd,
I keep telling myself.

I deserve a love that's true.

I deserve my cake and to eat it, too.

An option is what I've become.

He's not that into me.

No longer sprung.

I deserve a love that's true.

I deserve my cake and to eat it, too.

Dreams shattered wasted time.

So much for second chances.

Restoration was an illusion,

all to keep me wrapped in this ball of confusion.

I deserve a love that's true.

I deserve my cake and to eat it, too.

He'll never be mine.

I'm not a candidate for his mind, body and soul.

He's in control.

Shedding residue,

leaving casualties,

sowing seeds of mental brutality.

I deserve a love that's true.

I deserve my cake and to eat it, too.

I can't say I wasn't warned.

He showed me on the first take.

So be kind and rewind.

I deserve a love that's true.

I deserve my cake and to eat it, too.

Same old scene.

What I deserve remains to be seen.

Singing about falling in love at first sight.

Meanwhile, your presence has took a permanent flight.

Hijacked my heart and buried it in the sand.

Thanking my heavenly Father

because this was all a part of His master plan.

I deserve a love that's true.

I deserve my cake and to eat it, too.

Positioning me for the one I deserved,

no reason to look back.

Seasons change.

Thought this would last a lifetime,

in hope that my girls would have a peace of mind.

I deserve a love that's true.

Waiting patiently on my Father to deliver

the one who will be true.

About **WARRIORS TALK, Inc.**

Warriors Talk, Inc. NFP Est. 2014

I gave birth to Warriors Talk, Inc. In October 2014, as I began to share my testimony and distribute information on breast cancer. The Warriors Talk platform encourages, educates, and empower individuals into action for a healthier lifestyle before, during, and after a cancer diagnosis.

Warriors Talk Weekly Radio Broadcast

The Warriors Talk Radio Broadcast is going on 4 years old. On the show, we address how cancer, as well as other diseases, are running rampant throughout our country and how we can MOVE FROM AWARENESS TOWARDS ACTION. Listeners walk away empowered, informed, and connected to services. We encourage all to not only survive but thrive.

The broadcast consists of interviews of warriors in battle, survivors, doctors, nurses, researchers and many more.

Many use the broadcast as a weekly support group that they can attend from the comfort of their homes. Tune in every Monday 6 p.m. CST to Facebook LIVE @warriorstalk1 or Intellectual Radio.

Annual Survivors Night of Reflection Gala

October 19, 2019, we celebrated our 4th annual "Survivors Night of Reflection Gala." This event allows survivors to reflect on their journey and express their gratitude for life. They can all share their experience, knowledge, and wisdom after conquering cancer. This night is our annual fundraiser for those currently in battle. Funds raised go to our Warriors in the Battle Fund. This fund is available to individuals in the midst of fighting cancer that need some assistance to bridge the gap financially so that they can concentrate on fighting and healing.

Battle Buddy Sacs

A portion of the funds is also used for Battle Buddy Sacs. These sacs are put together with items handpicked and distributed to cancer centers throughout the Chicago Metropolitan Area and surrounding suburbs where Warriors in battle will receive their treatment. The sacs contain items to relax the mind, reduce stress, calm fears and document their journey while keeping their minds on thriving and surviving.

Annual Paint & Dip

Fighting cancer is no easy task. Many Warriors rarely get a moment to enjoy the little things in life. This event was created to give the Warrior in battle a sense of serenity while on their cancer journey. Each Warrior has the opportunity to create their masterpiece while relaxing and releasing some of the stress associated with fighting cancer.

ALSO BY RESHELLE L. MATHENY

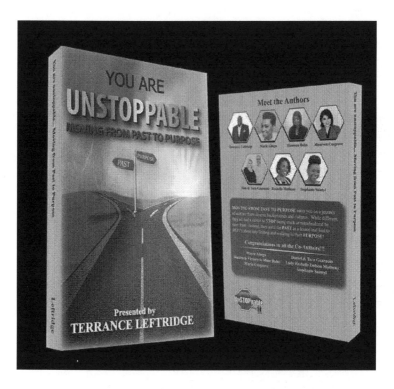

YOU ARE UNSTOPPABLE
MOVING FROM PAST TO PURPOSE
Takes you on a journey of from seven different
authors reflecting on their past storms that
attempted to STOP them from moving forward.
Although, they encounter different trials and
tribulations they used it as fuel to move PAST the
storm and walk into their PURPOSE
UNSTOPPABLE.

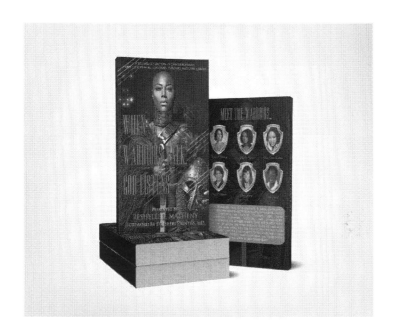

WARRIORS TALK, GOD LISTENS is a tell-all collection of cancer journeys from previvor, co-survivors, survivors and thrivers. The authors take you on their journey as they come face to face with their Goliath experience. This encounter tested them on every level, attempting to deplete their strength, faith, sanity and end their lives. Just as David did, they put on the whole armor of God and was successful at slaying their Giant. Sometimes we are weighed down with the pressures of life, rendering us helpless but one encounter with God can change the course of your journey.

 *Reshelle L. Matheny* is the Founder of Warriors Talk, Inc. NFP Est. 2014. As a Cancer Ambassador, she educates the community on the importance of cancer risks, early detection, and knowing your family history.

She currently hosts a weekly radio show 'Warriors Talk' that empowers individuals into action for a healthier lifestyle before, during, and after a cancer diagnosis.

Warriors Talk, Inc. hosts an annual "Survivors Night of Reflection Gala" that honors survivors and Warriors in battle. "Battle Buddy Sacs" are also donated to cancer treatment centers for those fighting cancer.

Currently, she volunteers as an Education Ambassador for Bright Pink. The mission is to save the lives of women from breast and ovarian cancer by empowering women to live proactively at a young age.

She was selected and currently serves as a Ford Warrior in Pink Model of Courage. The mission is to provide cancer patients with more good days.

Additionally, she serves as a Community Volunteer with the American Cancer Society where she educates the community and supports the needs of cancer patients.

Here are some of Reshelle's accomplishments:

Serves as the Outreach Coordinator at Emanuel Church of God In Christ on the Westside of Chicago.

- Speaker
- Emcee
- Facilitator of workshops for community events

Co-Author of the book anthology "You Are Unstoppable Moving from Past to Purpose," released in the spring of 2018.

Curator and Coach for the Book Anthology "When Warriors Talk, God Listens," released in the fall of 2019.

Recipient of the D.A. Reed Sr. District 2019 Hidden Figure Award.

Recipient of 2019 Keeps the Faith to Survive Five Star-Survivor Award.

Recipient of the PBW 2019 Phenomenal Women in Community Service.

In her free time, she enjoys writing poetry as well as performing spoken word. She also spends time with her children taking in all the beautiful Chicago attractions.

For more information on having Reshelle as a speaker or workshop facilitator at your next event, please connect with her:

Facebook/warriorstalk1
Twitter: @warriorstalk1
Instagram: warriorstalk1
Warriorstalk1@gmail.com
Website: www.warriorstalk.org
YouTube: warriorstalkw/ladyReShell
Donations: Cash App: $warriorstalk

You are responsible for your own happiness. Never put your power to be happy in the hands of another. Remember, its starts and ends with you."
~Reshelle L. Matheny